# CORRESPONDENCE
# IN D MINOR

STEPHEN F. AUSTIN STATE UNIVERSITY PRESS

JAMES R. DENNIS

CORRESPONDENCE
IN D MINOR

*For Mary Jane,*

*Amor enim, sine qua nihil est!*

*Best regards!*

THIS BOOK IS COPY NO. 106 OF TWO HUNDRED FIFTY
MMXVI

CORRESPONDENCE IN D MINOR

LIBRARY OF CONGRESS CATALOGING IN PUBLIATION DATA:
DENNIS, JAMES R.
CORRESPONDENCE IN D MINOR / JAMES R. DENNIS
1. POETRY. 2. TITLE. 3. JAMES DENNIS.

FIRST EDITION: AUGUST 2016
978-1-62288-168-0

STEPHEN F. AUSTIN STATE UNIVERSITY PRESS
PO BOX 13007, SFA STATION, NACOGDOCHES, TX 75962
SFAPRESS@SFASU.EDU SFASU.EDU/SFAPRESS

*THESE POEMS, WITH ALL THEIR CRUDITIES, DOUBTS,*
*AND CONFUSIONS, ARE WRITTEN*
*FOR THE LOVE OF MAN AND*
*IN PRAISE OF GOD, AND I'D BE A DAMN FOOL*
*IF THEY WEREN'T.*

~ DYLAN THOMAS

# ACKNOWLEDGEMENTS

GRATEFUL ACKNOWLEDGEMENT IS DUE TO THE EDITORS OF THESE PUBLICATIONS,
IN WHICH SOME OF THIS BOOK'S POEMS FIRST APPEARED:
*ANALECTA*: "LETTER TO JUAN ESTRADA", "THE ALAMO HOTEL"
*REFLECTIONS*: "TONIGHT"
*SAN ANTONIO EXPRESS NEWS*: "FALLEN"

PROFOUND THANKS TO KIM VERHINES AND STEPHEN F. AUSTIN PRESS FOR
SELECTING THIS COLLECTION FOR PUBLICATION. MANY THANKS TO MY TEACHERS, DAVID WEVILL AND
BISHOP ROBERT HIBBS, AND TO GILLIAN COOK, NOEL CROOK, CLAUDIA MACEO, NANCY MANCINI,
AND ANDREW MORRISON FOR THEIR HELP AND ENCOURAGEMENT.
I AM FOREVER IN THE DEBT OF LANA RIGSBY AND CARMEN GARZA FOR THE DESIGN
AND TYPESETTING OF THIS WORK. I ALSO OFFER MY THANKS TO
ALL THE FRIENDS AND FAMILY WHO INSPIRED AND HELPED ME ALONG THE WAY.

# Contents

## I

# II

# III

I

Scientia

# A Villanelle on the Day of Your Death

John, I think of you often; the thinking is never quite done.
I remember our time together: that mad, metaphysical time.
It's Holy Week here, and the work has only begun.

I hope you know the Holy Sonnets have had a good run;
I remember them whenever I hear the church bells chime.
You told me, and now the tolling is never quite done.

The facile ideas were the ones that you shunned.
For us, it's much harder. I'm writing, but only part-time.
It's Holy Week here, and the work has only begun.

I'll avoid the easy play upon the easy word, and shun the pun.
That's a slippery slope up which I shall not climb
during *Sanctum Sabbati*, while the work has only begun.

Of all those who wrote beneath an English sun,
I miss you the most. Your death has reduced the depth of time.
But we remember you often. The remembering is never quite done,
especially in Holy Week, when the work has just begun.

1

# A Visit to Sister Sophia

Years ago, I went to visit Sister Sophia because the signs
outside her shop promised great wonders.
They advertised (that) she knew my past,
could see my future, and would heal my broken places.

Upon entering, the bells on the door rang behind me,
announcing a visitation, announcing an opportunity
for a chat with the spirit world. Her shop smelled of incense, spices,
potions, teas, and a hint of *cabrito* from the back room.

And there, she laid it all before me: my life, my ruminations,
my ruinations, my loves, and my tomorrows,
all splayed out on the card table in the dim candlelight in Lubbock, Texas.
There, Sister Sophia read the palm at the end of the mind.

*Fabulous!*

# Letter to Trotsky

*Insurrection is an art, and like all arts has its own laws.*
—Leon Trotsky

You don't know me, but we have a good deal in common,
although I never knew Lenin.
Like you, I would never have trusted Stalin.

You and I were both educated in Odessa,
and while I was never in prison there,
I did kind of make a mess of

things. We both appreciate the working man,
the plight of those who feed their families
through common work with common hands.

I have also spent time in London, although
I was there for a vacation and you,
having fled Siberia, were there in exile.

Like you, I might have been compelled to action
when the Palace Guard slaughtered good, decent, hungry people
on Bloody Sunday, and might have made the same decision.

I admire the photographs of you during these years:
pointed, intense, full of passion and determination.
All these events make clear that

in another time, we might have been friends
until 1918 or so. It's hard to overlook the bloodbath
thereafter, hard to see beyond the violence.

I'm a peacenik down deep, you see,
and we must part ways when you euphemize
and hint at tearing away or chopping off the bourgeoisie.

Even you, committed as you were, could not ignore the pain,
the blood, the prisons, the labor camps which you yourself brought about.
You had to see that, riding through history on a black, Bolshevik train.

Even if you were not involved in the slaughter of the children of the tsar,
that kind of rhetoric can lead to that kind of thing,
things being as things are.

Like you, I might have fallen for Frida had I been on the lam,
and after a torrid affair, she would probably ) might
have called me the "Old Man"

too. Anyway, we've both had our adventures in Mexico.
I, however, was never so deeply concerned with dialectical materialism.
But Mexico, it sounds so simple, I may have to go

back. Simple, except for that evening on the *Avenida Viena*,
when that wretched assassin, Ramón Mercader, planted
an ice axe deep within your *cabeza*.

I still hope that, in that land of matadors, cathedrals and *chiles*,
you might have moderated your tone, softened your views
on a lifetime worth of these historical necessities.

# From Babel's Tower

From this western distance
on this particular summer night,
these words will not bend to my will.
The traitors betray me: they struggle, they fight.

Quite some time ago I traveled here
across the River of Troublesome Wonder,
through the Desert of the Dissolute, and
over the Mountains of Ambiguous Thunder,
wondering, "Where the devil did I put that compass?"

I came as a student, to learn of their strange science:
of their geometry, accomplished without a point of reference;
of their silly mathematics without numbers; and
of their daylight astronomy, based purely on guesswork.

And now, like a mourner turns to his grief,
as a god turns to his time,
like a mother turns to her children,
as a drunkard turns to his wine,
my thoughts turn to them.

From their home, in the distant East,
I hear the stories of Chloe and Capitan.
"What are you doing?
What are your plans?"

As a fool returns to his folly,
as a workman returns to his toil,
like a sailor returns to his charts,
as a farmer returns to his soil,
my heart returns to them.

Here, in this western twilight,
I hear their voices, I feel her hands.
"What are you doing?
What are your plans?"

# Homage

*El original es infiel a la traducción.*
—Jorge Luis Borges

Into the evening, *ich und du,*
our destination laid before us: lines upon the map, a faded blue,
reveal themselves in flickering street lamps.
We proceed, cautiously at first, down dusty roads,
where once-inscrutable, now broken codes
divulge the meaning of sluggish argument
and the daily struggle to pay the rent.
We follow vapor trails of an old conversation
waiting, with diminished expectations,
pushed along to a crowded conclusion . . . .
Come, set aside your despair.
Let's return to another evening's affair.

The bawdy politics of small talk somehow
leave us breathlessly unimpressed right now.

The mist of tar and nicotine that wrapped around her face,
the smoky mist that coiled its length around her face,
stretched itself, end to end, across the evening,
passing the time in the corridors of that night,
gentle and silent, disturbing neither object nor moment
and then trundling across the lawn, reticent and shy,
but rising, dispersed toward an unforgiving moon.
Lingering there, it dissipated carelessly into the Hill Country sky.

And of course we will make room
for that odd, imperious mist as it leaks into the landscape
wrapping itself, coiling around her face.
We will make room, we will make room:
a space for hello and for goodbye, and how do you do.
Room enough to work and a place to sit idle,
room enough for sinner and saint,
room enough for god and idol.
Room for yours and room for mine
and for a thousand small-time portrayals

and for a thousand lesser angels and betrayals
before the cheese and before the wine.

The bawdy politics of small talk somehow
leave us breathlessly unimpressed right now.

And of course, we will find a space
to inquire, "Could I do it?" and "Could I do it?"
Room enough to see the window and to see through it,
with a paragraph progressing well enough until in the final line I blew it—
("A shame," they said, "he showed such promise in his prime.")
This denim jacket, tattered here and there enough to make it mine,
these leather boots, a rough gloss reveals a bit of shine—
(But they observe, "He showed such promise in his prime.")
Could I do it
in the moment when it mattered?
In that instant could I portray all that I intended
without the need to later amend it, in a subsequent revision of my thought.

This night is like every other night, like every other night:
I understand their dinners, their functions, their cocktail parties.
I have known their Sherlock Holmes' and known their Moriarties.
I know the laughter that within reveals a sudden bite
with just a toss of the hair, or a flash of spark within the eyes.
        And how can we proceed?

This night is like all the nights, like every other night—
evenings that wrap around you tightly like a bandage,
and once bound, you squirm against their gaze,
tossing back the whiskey, avoiding the light.
Eyes that search you to appraise
the clever repartee which we have failed to manage.
        And how can we proceed?

This particular evening is like all the rest, like every other night—
eyes that dance a waltz from this person to that
(but begin to drop as discourse is reduced to chat).
I wonder, watching her breasts rise and fall

if I am trapped in this cabal?
Eyes inviting my company, or calling me to fight or flight.
      And how can we proceed?
      And how can we commence?

Shall we mention we have read this book or that,
covered topics well which would escape most folks' attention
and smelled the smoke which drifts above a glass of cabernet.

We should abide in a Petri dish,
floating in an agar mix, waiting for a bit of culture.

But the garden, the lawn, stretches out across the horizon.
Against the sound of boots upon the flagstone path
I calculate the clatter in drunken math.
Remind me about the Doppler effect again, *paisan.*
Might we, after beer and chips and *queso*
bring the moment to a head on our own say-so?
Although we have removed our boots and had our feet washed there,
(you remember the room above and the dinner, a little time alone)
we are no apostles—we are common flesh and common bone.
I have developed the habit of failing to impress,
I have watched the academics chuckle as I stumble and digress,
and I have known the terror of the whole affair.

And in the final analysis, after all is said and all is done,
once the dishes have been swept away
and the conversation takes a turn, then turns astray,
we spare ourselves this discursive alchemy.
We prepare our assault, a cocktail party mutiny:
to hoist the black flags, raise them one by one,
to hear them flapping in the evening's breeze
and announce: "I have seen the Ghost Dance on the lawn,
the Spirits rising up to join the fun."
And the hostess, smiling at me with a little tease,
      asserts, "This is not how things are done,
      not how things are done."

And in the final analysis, after some is lost and some is won,
having considered this and considered that,
once the neighbors' lights are out and doors are locked,
having finished with the music for the night,
ending this, and all delight—
despite the offer to help with the cleaning,
my reputation suffers, beyond redeeming.
Having considered this, and considered that,
if she, teasing a bit when the evening's gone,
should look in our direction
          and say, "This is not how things are done,
          not how things are done."

I cannot see myself as Colonel Travis—no, not at all,
although I might have ridden out for help some starless night
avoiding Santa Anna's sentries, and abstaining from the fight.
No hero, and yet a task to do, a role to play:
stealthy, cunning to a certain extent,
not a martyr, but joining in the struggle.
Not rushing forward, but offering my assent,
and on occasion, a bit befuddled,
and ready, now and then, to run away.

This is boring, this is boring.
I'm not sure we're even worth ignoring.

Perhaps I'll drink tequila. Perhaps we'll go, my brother,
and make our camp in the Balcones.
I have heard the coyotes howling one to another,

I doubt they'll howl for us.

I have watched them hunt in pairs,
creeping through the brush at night,
perhaps an instinct, perhaps a second sight.

We have wandered through these plains without a compass that we trust,
until the dawn breaks, revealing that this is no common ground.
And we are lost, and we are lost, and we are nowhere to be found.

## HAEMON REMEMBERS

We shared our time, our land, our tribe.
Woven together, those longings swam

along that distant shore.
Now, absent her, those ancient passions

conspire with my failing nerve.
What crimes are these we answer for?

One afternoon, beneath an olive tree,
all this passed between Antigone and me.


The chorus now makes clear
that hubris uncentered our lives,

and mocked the rage of savage gods.
Somehow, we earned her brutish grave.

Who could have known?
What were the odds?

We cursed our time, our tribe and Thebes
and held so close, Antigone and me.


Hoping for time to reimburse these losses and
forgive these debts, I watch the boats come and go.

I wait and know she will not return.
Cautious, politic, and well informed,

my recollection lies in lines I've learned
and the corners I have turned.

We laughed that night at the jubilee;
we'll not laugh again, Antigone and me.

## Isaac, To His Father

Let's talk about the elephant in the room, Pops,
about that afternoon. Me, happily carrying a bundle of wood:
I can still hear it, the rough crunch of rocks
under our feet. Flesh of your flesh, blood of your blood.
So long ago, the years have sipped away my strength
like good wine, and clouded my eyes.
But I recall, with mathematical precision, the length
of that walk, the stark bright sun, and the bitter echo of my cries.
I wanted you to save me, to spare me, but you had something else in mind.
The sacrifice, you see, does not see a priest; the sacrifice sees a butcher.
From my viewpoint, this single-minded obedience was a bit less than kind.
At that moment, I set all questions of parenting aside, both nature and nurture.
As we climbed, you might have shared that my tense would soon be past.
"The Lord will provide the lamb," my ass.

## The Alamo Hotel

The night clerk is a friend,
a good friend. He gives me coffee
and we smoke these old cigarettes until it's late.
We'll be talking until the decaying southern man
who wears a grey suit announces breakfast,
and we'll both leave then.

The night clerk is studying when he has the time.
Then he reminds me of the history of this place,
and the extraordinary phenomena
which become clear when the moon
is full and the night air is thick and wild.

I'm fiddling around with the Western Union typewriter,
his books, and the wooden box of keys.
Or I'm reading the magazines and medical journals,
thinking about the wandering dance of ghosts
which haunts some times, places and people.

Old George comes down from his room,
of two minds, like Jonah, and says, "You hear me?
Maybe Persia is an old woman and she can crochet
but would rather attend festivals. Like smelly waters.
You hear me? You two might take to the bottle:
if you've lost, then what you've ensconced is a city."
And then he heads back up to his room.
While George walks up the staircase he tells us,
"Play on, ye soft pipes."

The desk clerk looks at me and says,
"We aren't understanding
these desecrated burial grounds,
but are swimming in whirlpools."

Later, on leaving the hotel,
standing on 6th street
we notice the harvest moon
like primitives or farmers in the Dakotas,
thinking of tides or the rain,
fields and women.
Now, watching the light,
the white glow is bent and split
into all colors we can see.

## The Least Obvious Evil Possible

*During peacetime, a scientist belongs to the World, but during wartime,*
*he belongs to his country.*
—Fritz Haber

At the second battle of Ypres,
we learned what you had been doing in your lab,
you little devil, you, despite the Hague Convention
of nineteen hundred and seven.
There in Kitchener's Wood
this was no manna that fell down from heaven.
No, with lungs set afire, the French crawled
along the ground like blinded crabs.

And you wanted to see it for yourself,
after the disappointing outcome
on the Russian front,
where the bromide tear gas froze.
You wanted to see it for yourself,
strutting around in your new patriotic clothes.
You wanted to see it, to watch the chemical spray
from this deadly fountain.

And you succeeded
in the development of Haber's Rule:
reducing suffering and death
to an algorithm,
taking the guess work out of it,
removing all the indecision.
You were nobody's fool, Haber,
nobody's fool.

Clara could not bear
what you had done,
or perhaps could not abide
her restrictive role as the bride
of Lucifer's alchemist

and by her own hand she died.
It was her hand, but your service revolver,
by which she was undone.

I have heard your defense
of your work:
the argument that death is death and
the method is of no consequence.
Perhaps, like Faust, you would someday
learn your work's provenance.
And of course, it wasn't just you.
The whole bloody world had gone berserk.

Thinking of the science of food production,
they later gave you the Prize,
recognizing your work in the synthesis
of ammonia from common gasses.
Can science ever be value-free?
Can any study avoid morality's forty lashes?
Even if we could,
should act and consequence ever be untied?

How then do we measure the value of a man;
how do we weigh the balance of a life?
Do we look at the good left behind
or the pain that was caused?
Do we examine the average, the mean,
or is this where all judgment withdraws?
One cannot remove hubris
with a surgical knife.

I think I'll ask someone else.
You're not my first choice.
I didn't mention the attempt
to extract gold from sea water.
It seems a bit silly now, but no sillier
than turning breath into death or the slaughter
of all those boys,
all those boys.

# Elegy for Elmer

Before he came to Hollywood, with a suitcase full of dreams,
a bulbous nose and his thespian schemes;

Before he left his hometown, before the lonely bus ride out of Pittsburgh,
before the classes in Hell's Kitchen, where he studied under Strasberg;

Before the hunting jacket and the shotgun blasts combined
to render him a bad punch line, a goofball in a duck blind;

Before he spiraled down, before the studio insisted he see a doctor,
before his pathological insistence on singing the music of Richard Wagner;

Before the torrid affair with a starlet, before the dimming of his art,
before he became a laughing stock, which broke his widdle heart;

Before the women and the booze and pills and the scandal sheets,
the lesser parts, the cut-rate scripts and a thousand surreptitious retreats;

Before squandering his poor talents on unspeakable acts of decadence,
he was just a kid. Just a kid, with a speech impediment.

## William Bonny Writes Pat Garret

Aside from my life among these ninnies, *compadre*,
all goes splendidly. *Ellos son muy amables.*

The furtive smiles, the narcoleptic days,
the internecine nights and conspiratorial praise—

all these available to the desperado for hire,
laughing and leaping from frying pan to fire.


Harmonia hauled ass last spring, and left without a tear.
I have forgotten her touch, but remember her fair

skin. Sometimes in my dreams, I still see her face.
Pat, I have grown tired of this place.

Ten years ago, I arrived to help these folk—their old, their young.
and I have fought in their war against their native tongue.


I have carried their load; I have done all their chores.
I have drunk their bitter beer and have known all their whores.

I have suffered ten years in this miserable weather,
Watched the horses return, seen the blood on the leather.

But I will quit this struggle and abandon this strife.
I am leaving these morons to get on with my life.


The townspeople speak of a price on my head;
the governor and landowners all want me dead.

I am done with this place, done with the cattle and saguaro.
I am no cowboy, nor a shopkeeper, but a passable *pistolero.*

These are important facts, Pat, that I have learned.
Why don't you meet me in the Valley of the Unconcerned?

## Numen

There is this red coffee can
full of half-forgotten ideas and distant music:
it sits rusting on a limestone ridge
in Comal County.

But that is not the worst of it.
      "Talk about the moonlight;
        Tell them about the moonlight."
I was just getting to that.

At night, the dead walk along the Balcones Escarpment: Apaches, Tonkawa,
ghosts of Spanish missionaries, German immigrants, farmers and ranchers.
They bring their gifts, their airy *ofrendas,* and lay them near:
songs and sounds, words and bits of light.

Through forces no science can comprehend,
this old coffee can draws the landscape to itself. The sparse clouds,
the live oak, the deer, the black-chinned hummingbird,
the wild goats, the Blanco River: all caught up in a Hill Country vortex.

To forestall the ruinous consequence of time, this teeming can lies sealed
under a glass case. (Those having seen Lenin's tomb will remark on the similarities.)
Unlike Pandora's jar, no troubles will take flight from here:
no furies fly from this place, nor are they welcome in this county.

At times, this well-worn can seems almost human
like a monk in some scriptorium with a bad back
going over all he can see and forever muttering,
*"Ni modo, nihil obstat."*

There is this red coffee can,
trying to forget the past.

II

QUALIA

# FALLEN

*You may freely eat of every tree of the garden;*
*but of the tree of the knowledge of good and evil you shall not eat . . . .*
—Genesis 2: 16–17

Whatever the regulations or the guidelines were,
we disregarded them.
I can't even remember what it was:
perhaps something to do with produce
or vegetation or trees or whatever.
The facts are resistant to our recollection.
And now we wander, refugees of a sort,
with sacks on our backs, carrying not our belongings
but our regret. And I'm not sure we'll ever find the way home.
We carry the burden of an intimacy disentangled,
finding this new knowledge a little less than ken,
a little less than kind. Compelled to travel:
crowded, not into a smaller place,
but a much larger geography.
There is plenty of land here,
but so little room to maneuver.

# TECHNOLOGY

My computer will not communicate with the printer, leading
me to wonder if I have stumbled upon some ancient squabble,
some blood feud that arose long ago, before I knew either of them.
This could result in years of complicated legal proceedings.

The trouble might be of a political nature, arising from anarchist's pistol shot,
and all the accessories will click into place, alliances based upon geography
and familial collaborations. Perhaps this is only the spark that will spread
to all my electronics, and maybe even the appliances that I have bought.

This could have arisen from some sort of religious failing:
like Zechariah, the computer has been struck dumb
for disregarding its better angels.
And now, against a firewall, they all are wailing.

Or possibly this conflict springs from a romance gone wrong;
the computer overheard the printer whispering to the scanner
in a hushed and tender voice, ignoring her betrothal,
forgetting to whom she belonged.

And now, they will not speak at all, they will not share their ones and zeroes.
And I am caught between them, as they shout insults and mock each other
here on the hot gates of this electronic Thermopylae. But I find no Xerxes,
and no Leonidas here—on this battlefield, there are no heroes.

Perhaps, after giving in time and again to the computer's caprice,
after years of oppression and doing the digital heavy-lifting around here,
the printer has risen up in some sort of Marxist revolution.
And the sullen device murmurs, "No justice, no peace."

# LETTER TO JUAN ESTRADA

*John Graham was a stock broker in Dallas, Texas.*
*One day, he decided to leave that life altogether and walked away from his career,*
*his home, and his family. When I met him around 1980, he had changed his name*
*to Juan Ezekiel Estrada, III. Juan lived on his boat, the Mauna Loa,*
*although the motor of that noble craft never functioned to my knowledge.*
*He had filled it (beyond all reason and all capacity) with junk*
*and other detritus he found around the bay in Rockport.*

*Nombre nuevo*
You are reminding me that we do not choose our thoughts
that misnomer occurs in many instances
        I have to tell you that it is only recently
        that I have begun to enjoy this city

Seeing you, thinking of seeing you
        and realizing that I am not
        the packrat I thought I was
Always about to wear another pair of spectacles
        they spoke of an early repair, Juan

You live on a boat, another
        less than seaworthy vessel
and know everyone around the bay
        the shrimpers and the vacationing businessmen
In the evening we watched television and drank beer
        until the cable was broken
        and I thought I had become endemic
While the redfish were biting
you talked about the other storms and family,
        a delta of the mind

*Nombre nuevo, hombre nuevo*
You make it clear that all recent history
begins within you
        You said we often find
        ourselves unattached, on the water

## AHAB, TO HIS WIFE

You've got a lot of goddamned nerve, darling,
asking me to show a little Christian charity.

Do you think I do not know I have become a maimed caricature
of myself? Asking every passing ship, "Hast thou seen him?

Hast thou seen the white whale?" Do you not think
I know what a bother I've become?

> For we are all killers,
> out of our pain, soft-peddling our glee.
> For we are all killers,
> on land and on sea.

But I will follow this devil,
follow him round the Cape of Degradation,

across the Sea of Blasphemy
and into Satan's Maelstrom itself.

I will follow this demon that rendered me
nothing more than a seagoing footnote.

> For we are all killers,
> out of our pain, concealing our glee.
> For we are all killers,
> on land and on sea.

For the sake of hatred, I will bear these islands,
and their smelly, tattooed barbarians.

For the sake of hatred, I will endure
that sacred loss of life, limb and pride.

Where was this Christ of yours while I suffered?
Did he find himself otherwise occupied?

For we are all killers,
out of our pain, veiling our glee.
For we are all killers,
on land and on sea.

So, regarding your request for Christian charity,
until I have slaked my thirst for vengeance,

until this account has been squared
and my wrath measured to the penny,

until he spouts black blood and I hear
his cries from Perdition, don't ask again.

# In His City

Those spirits we stumbled upon dancing yesterday evening
were simply the residue of something delivered up long ago.
Of this much, I am convinced.

They were not devils, but familiars grown distant and old.
Some beat small stones together, lit fires, cursed loudly,
took no food. And, watching the central fire spread
during the hornpipe, in a sense, I was consumed.

But seven nights later, without caesurae, I was in the arms
of my favorite. She read to me about Augustine and his apology.
While reading, she marked me with a hot ash.

For a while I could do nothing but listen and stare at those stone walls.
Then I told her, "We had an idea of time unfolding,
a schema or wire grid extending for miles based on one assumption:
that other systems were possible.
The entire network collapsed beneath us
when we saw that we were mistaken."

As I spoke to her of a flowering in history,
she asked me to account for several possible digressions.
Among them, some geographer, shot in the head by a close friend,
and deciding he could compromise on the continuity of his spirit,
he walks around like Lazarus with powder burns
on his temple. He is broken and becomes a man again.
Seeing she didn't understand and had begun to undress,
I wondered if we could change the subject.

This refused me, and thinking
beyond that city and its stone walls
the hornpipe was still sounding,
troubled with ideas of a god who destroys
everything he has begun to understand,
I walked to find a field in which were enclosed
several small gardens and met a cleric
who called himself the groundskeeper.
He told me his real interest lay in natural astronomy,
listening to the planets turning and grinding out their orbits,
perfect circles in the divine wind,
and their harmony.
He said, "I believe we are seeing old light.
And there is something else, something more abstract."

# Necessity

We are given a land becoming dry,
a land in drought, or a wooden fence.
And all our notions follow these.

Imagine Christ, telling us to cast our nets
to the other side, and you slander
the brute fact of the adequate fence.

My father rode a line of rotten old fence
like this, in a hard country where
dust and sand are the *idée fixe.*

This land aches
for rain, as we ache
for meaning, for a narrative.

Reason dwells within the land—
spills into the bone-dry afternoon sky.

Not simply placed upon this property,
we are woven into the landscape.

## ORDINARY TIME

After that first not so original sin
we were given the original boot.
From that time until now, a quarter past ten

on an April night as my patience grows thin,
we still struggle with that tragic bit of forbidden fruit.
After that first, not so original sin . . . .

Through this advent we have sought after Emmanuel, our friend:
a message of hope that our drudgery would not mute.
From that time until now, a quarter past ten

we have waited, thoughtfully stroking our chinny-chin-chin.
Where is our epiphany? Where is our spiritual loot?
After that first not so original sin

we built a temple, thinking we might win
His affection. But, regarding that architecture, He did not give a hoot.
From that time until now, a quarter past ten

We have sung our Easter alleluias, now and then
and dressed in our new Pentecostal pinstriped suit.
After that first not so original sin,
from that time until now, a quarter past ten . . . .

# All Hallows' Eve, 2015

## I.

*Eye of newt and toe of frog, wool of bat and tongue of dog.*
—William Shakespeare

It's not to ghouls, goblins, ghosts or werewolves.
No, tonight, my thoughts have turned to witches: the "witches"
of Salem, in particular, to Cotton Mather, to possessions,
the Old Deluder, enchantments and that sort of business.

I suppose the original impulse was all right.
They wanted to improve the world, to purify the ills
of humankind and the church. But we all know
who makes his home in the details.

They made their way in a climate of fear:
pervasive, ubiquitous fear was the crook they could not straighten.
Famine, pestilence, the Wakanabi tribe, the battle for their souls,
and worst of all, they confronted Satan.

They were convinced of an invisible reality,
a reality apparent to all "ingenious men,"
convinced of demons, angels, conjurers:
and all this securely within their ken.

This was more than a simple pastime,
a diversion from that brutal New England climate.
Nor was this some miasma, foul humor, troublesome zeitgeist
or something like that: these trials were not aberrant

at all. No, from time to time,
we mortal men do this kind of thing.
We succumb to our lesser angels, give into the terrors
of living together, and wait for the hell-hounds to sing.

# II.

*A witch is born out of the true hungers of her time.*
—Ray Bradbury

Between 1692 and 1693, the difficulties began to reveal themselves
in Salem Town, Ipswich, Andover and Salem Village.
They were an interesting lot: mostly literate and inexhaustibly literal
and it was a kind of collective forgetting of the image

in which they were made. Perhaps they revealed
the flaw of Calvinism: its soft, pale underbelly.
Constantly examining themselves and their sin,
looking for signs of their total depravity.

It's a small step, you see, from the notion
that mankind is totally depraved to the claim
that my neighbor, or my wife, or my minister
is full of evil and thus enslaved

to the Devil, to Old Scratch. It was an odd time: cold, ashen skies,
smoky and pervasive darkness. New England was less enchanting then
and more enchanted. A world without brightness or color,
save varying shades of darkness, thinly lit and when

they had to explain their troubles (the dead horse, the plague,
the crop loss, the mad dog, the crackpot on the corner),
conjurers offered a ready, if not especially reliable,
explanation for blight, disease, trouble or horror.

They carved out a home in a world that resisted
their intelligence, but easily accommodated
their dread of things that go bump
in the night: Wakanabi scalping parties, the well-hated

French, Catholics, goblins, toads that drank blood,
and the despised wiles and devices of our Ancient Enemy, bent
on the ruin of God's kingdom in New England.
Aside from the struggle of daily life, their leisure was spent

in the timid study of God's holy word.
Perhaps they knew each other too well
to believe in heaven or a generous God,
but they could easily embrace the notion of the flames of hell.


III.

*The number of witches everywhere had become enormous.*
—John Jewell


The accusers, those who bore witness, were an odd lot.
They can be roughly divided into those who had been "harmed,"
those who had confessed and were thus compelled to name names,
and the afflicted (including the girls who seemed to have charmed

the magistrates), whose antics occupied the trials. These girls, these shrieking girls
(servants mostly), call upon us to draw, or at least consider, the fine line
between hysteria, a lie, a delusion, a craving for attention, and the possibility
(or the possibility of a possibility) that they really saw some sort of sign

of something. The girls barked like dogs, jumped about like frogs,
purred like kittens and flapped their arms like birds.
One could not avoid the conviction
of the insufficiency of comfort, prayer, or any words.

How could the godly rest?
How could a holy people take a moment's leisure
while these girls struggled against invisible chains
and wallowed and writhed in serpentine seizures?

Among the victims of the malicious felony of witchcraft,
husbands testified against their wives, daughters against their mothers,
neighbor bore witness against neighbor, and congregant against minister.
Further, siblings swore out their oaths against each other.

It's hard to know how they regarded their own fanciful testimony,
whether at some place in their hearts they believed themselves to be on the level.
Perhaps they simply sought to preserve themselves as they swore,
"I saw Sarah Osborne speaking with the devil."

They spoke of magic most dark: frozen cattle, the pricks of unseen pins,
bewitched hay, diabolical distempers, cankerous boils,
and unholy visits to their bedrooms in the night.
Surely, the diabolical arts were practiced on that New England soil.

The lives of confessed witches were generally spared
once they swore that they had written their own names in Satan's book,
and testified to the late-night rides into a darkened sky, identified their accomplices
and those at the Black Mass, and described how the devil undertook

to take them all, every one, to hell. Witchcraft seemed
to run in families, although some would hardly show it—
an inherited trait, passed from generation to generation.
Even the most saintly had to wonder: "Could I be a witch and not know it?"


IV.

*You shall not suffer a witch to live.*
—Exodus 22:18


The numbers of those falling victim
to "the disease of astonishment" are telling:
over a hundred forty-four were named as warlocks and witches.
fifty five of them confessed, compelling

one to scratch one's head. In 1692, in Massachusetts Bay
five men, fourteen women and two dogs were executed.
History does not record the breed of the dogs,
although I suspect terriers were among the persecuted.

(I am personally acquainted with this: terriers are
particularly susceptible to demonic possession. But I digress.
On the other hand, from a procedural point of view,
I don't think either of the dogs confessed.)

The evidence against them was overwhelming:
they could not recite the Lord's Prayer, had the power of the evil eye
muttered too loudly ("Satan's music"), bore the blemish of the Beast,
possessed poppets of wax or rags, or the "afflicted" saw them whisk by

in the air. They called such testimony "spectral evidence"
And it served to convict many of those witches in the dock.
Modern mystics might call it a vision, modern psychologists
might view it as hallucinatory, and modern jurists as poppycock.

The vast majority of those convicted hung, twenty in all (mostly women)
who conspired in the molestations of the invisible world.
As they rode, then walked up to Gallows Hill, some prayed,
hopeful of a late deliverance, while others hurled

curses at the eager crowd. For refusing to stand trial "by God
and my country" Old Giles Corey may have had it the worst.
In the *peine forte et dure*, they crushed him under stones for several days
and excommunicated him twice, while the elements and his thirst

consumed him. But in some sense, they were all consumed.
Fear can make a meal of any of us, as it did of them.
Terror is a funny thing: some folks run from it
and others go looking for it, again and again.

# V.

*I find your lack of faith disturbing.*
—Darth Vader

So, tonight, my doorbell rang again and again
and I had a vision: I heard small voices in high pitches:
I saw vampires, zombies, devils and ghouls,
and, of course, there had to be witches.

I did not call the constable nor seek to convene a trial.
I do not believe they are in league with the Prince of Hell.
They do not frighten me, nor am I especially concerned for their souls
although the mob frightens me, and sometimes I frighten myself as well.

No, we are a more reasoned people:
we have balances, balances and checks.
We would no longer dare to go off half-cocked
and round up the usual suspects.

Tonight, I have exhausted my interest in the supernatural.
Although there are plenty of signs, I have no sense
of evil in their hearts or of the dark arts in this neighborhood.
However, I have some concerns about the orange cat on my neighbor's fence.

Tonight, there are no devils or demons afoot:
not in the houses, on the lawns, or on the sidewalks.
The Old Deluder holds no sway on Hacienda Trail,
and that suggestion—well, that's crazy talk.

# The Hippopotamus

*In the Third Common Era of Absentia, a scholar named Elliot the Lesser*
*studied at the Library of Babel. While there, within the Library's Encyclopaedia,*
*he read an article concerning the beast (which virtually all academics*
*now consider mythical) called the "hippopotamus." Devoting the balance of*
*his scholarly efforts to the study of this creature, his obscure works*
*thereafter can only generously be described as "distracted."*
*His notes from that initial encounter follow here.*

From the Greek, meaning "river horse," the ancient creature
first appeared during the Post-Despondent Period.
Territorial in the extreme, she spends her days
in the River of Ambivalence.

The creature, rumored to frighten demons,
appears passive and clumsy.
Unpredictable and quick to anger, however,
the graceful hippo fiercely protects her own.

The calf, born under the water, struggles to swim
to the surface for its first gasp of air. Often nursing
beneath the water, the young hippo spends the bulk
of its aquatic days, however, on its mother's back.

The hippopotamus will travel great distances
to establish her natural grazing lands.
Through the misty African nights,
she travels alone and fearlessly.

The hippo can remain under water for over six years,
during which time its heart rate slows.
At the river, they gather in herds of twenty or more,
and will leave the river's bed only in established, well-worn paths.

The thin skin of the hippopotamus often appears purple
in color because the hippo (a fact not widely known)
sweats either blood or wine. Her soft brown eyes often
reveal nothing other than a snobbish sort of disdain.

The bellicose hippopotamus speaks with God,
in the language of prehistoric beasts.
Ancient man sought to live among them,
drunkards mostly, who met with no success.

On cool nights, as the hippo rises from her pool,
the mythic moonlight glistens on her skin.
As the steam rises from her flesh, the beast smiles,
But her eyes flash with rage as she gambles away the night.

The song of the hippopotamus is addictive,
and foolish men often long for her touch,
asking if the hippopotamus notices them.
The  hippo answers, "Not so much."

# A Confession for My Brother

If you will remain a while longer, *hermano,*
if you will but sit here with me in the early sun's glow

if you will remain here, near the hills around Raleigh
I promise to confess all of my folly.

I have traveled down the Corridors of Repetition,
I have bathed in the Waters of a Senseless Condition.

I have ridden the Horses of the Narrow Pass
and dwelt in the House of Logic's Morass.

All that is finished.


I should have written earlier, and been more clever.
I should have paid more attention to this disastrous weather.

I should have fought in the War of Giggly Insurrection
and honored Our Lady of Immaculate Correction.

Your mother, Our Lady, still grieves for our losses
praying to Jude, the Saint of Lost Causes.

All that is finished.


I have dined with dissolution
(I have carefully) avoided all absolution.

I have drunk from the Well Where Wisdom Is Lost
and counted the money, while ignoring the cost.

I have written four letters that never were sent
and prayed with no intent to repent.

All that is finished.

I have eked out a life in this foreign dirt.
Spilling their wine, I have stained this classic shirt.

Embracing chaos, I cursed an ancient race.
I have retired to my quarters in this drunken place.

I have rolled away the stone, and found an empty tomb.
I have gone for months without cleaning my room.

All that is finished.


Now, I have something to say to you
as the thinking of god becomes smoky dew.

So then, in your discontented and failing state
I propose a bargain as evidence that I am not afraid.

I will wage war, and fight like the great hero Cú Chulainn
if you will stay here, if you will but remain.

## DEUS ABSCONDITUS

Across the stone floor,
through the parted sea of wooden benches,
he approached that naked tree,

that intersection. Missing its incumbent,
The upright and transverse branches
lent no intimation that they ever bore humanity.

He turned and knelt there
at the altar of repose, vigilant
and stripped of all consequence.

Years before, long before
he had the vocabulary or the edifice of thought
upon which to hang the notion, he had felt the Presence.

Now these collects rise up,
from matins to compline.
They mingle and then dissipate.

"What exactly," he wonders,
"do You want? Were we,
perhaps, mistaken? How long should I wait?"

The candles flicker at the sacred cabinet.
Whether incarnate or transcendent,
nothing becomes manifest—no sacred whatnot.

No one speaks, no one makes their presence known.
At the darkened altar, he waits for the revelation which is there
within the revelation which is not.

## Letter to a Russian Jew

If you return, would you go for a walk with me while the evening
falls around us, cool and familiar like a fine satin sheet?
We could amble through the park by the alstroemeria,
or drive to the café on the cobblestone streets.

We could go to the Garden of Eden and re-name
all the beasts. I hear the fresh produce there is great.
It all depends upon your mood: if you prefer we could
take the train to Tunisia and sleep late.

There, in the land of Berbers, we could go down to the sea.
We could take our coffee at mid-morning and watch the light
darting through the alleys. In Bizerte, they make cakes with geranium water.
I remember laughing at the waiter with the notorious overbite.

We might make our way to Zambia,
wearing khakis and sunglasses and watch the birds at sunset.
I have thought of the landmarks; I remember them all.
I remember the crocodile and recall the egret.

Down the Zambezi River, we might hunt
for your perfect day. I am certain it still remains.
Or we could go for a drive across the Serengeti and wait
for the sun to rise through the scrub on the African plains.

You might rather go to Rome and taste the tomatoes and olives.
We could look for signs of the martyrs in the ruins of stone.
There is something so baroque about the evenings there:
in the center lies the Mediterranean weather and the Papal dome.

We could return to the Sangre de Cristo Mountains and tell ghost stories
or linger in the bakery after lunch when the plates are taken away.
They say that the pastries whisper about politics when everyone is gone.
They discuss the news, the rumors, and the remnants of the day.

We could ponder Jane Goodall's study of chimps,
or pass an entire afternoon with three chess moves.
We could talk about polio, the Alamo, or the villainy of Cossacks.
We might speak of chemistry or of mysteries or of things to improve.

In your absence, I have heard the wind
in the chimes and seen the boats in the moonlight.
It has been too long, old friend, but I cannot forget.
And I cannot squeeze any more from my recollections, try as I might.

I remember your smile,
sometimes ambrosial and sometimes obscure.
And if you come back I promise
to never again use any literary lure.

We could sail to Crete or hike in the Alps,
watch the horses in Kentucky or examine the temples in Kathmandu.
I leave this to your discretion. I do not care where we go;
I do not care what we do.

# III

Nihil

# Tonight

Tonight, I don't want to sit with the dying anymore.
I do not want to watch their families or see the struggle in their eyes.
I cannot bear to walk through another oncology ward.

Tonight, I do not want to pray for those who have been lost anymore.
I do not want to try and out-ride the black cares that chase me through the night.
I do not want to find myself falling into some broken-hearted trap door.

Tonight, I do not want to pray for the unthinkable, to beseech against long odds.
I do not want to kneel, or to take up the heavy string of beads
I do not want to wonder whether heaven spurns or heaven nods.

Tonight, I do not want to hold a hand as the airways begin to constrict.
I do not want to think about what lies beyond or silent heaven's promise.
I cannot do much more. The pocket where I kept my resolve has been picked.

Tonight, I do not want to know about the tumor's metastasis or reduction.
I do not want to stare out the window, or swear a curse in the parking lot.
I do not want to think about the silent grave's seduction.

Tonight, I do not want to listen to the breathing as the lungs begin to fill,
Or the chatter in the hallways as the wishes of the patient and the family are weighed.
But tomorrow, despite my clumsy tongue and artlessness, tomorrow I will.

## Eppur Si Muove

*In September of 1632, Galileo Galilei was summoned to Rome and*
*brought before the inquisitor Vincenzo Maculani. Galileo faced charges because of*
*his heretical opinions that the sun remained motionless at the center of the universe, and*
*that the earth (which was thus not at the center of the universe) moved around the sun.*
*Ultimately, Galileo recanted these positions, but was nevertheless found*
*"vehemently suspect of heresy" and sentenced to imprisonment at the pleasure of the Inquisition.*
*According to legend, although he had recanted his heretical views, upon leaving*
*the proceeding Galileo muttered, "Eppur si muove" (And yet, it moves).*

The real question before us, the trouble as we study creation and its clues,
is what lies at the center of things. The earth must remain still and taut.
And yet, it moves.

This study was simple. I did not seek to uncover some scriptural ruse—
only to observe that which was mutable and that which was not.
The real question, apparently, was not what but who.

I just looked through the glass, and observed a few truths,
"The world is firmly established and cannot . . . ."
And yet, it moves.

Deny it all! What have you got to lose?
Call a coarse thing fine. Call it fresh, despite the rot.
Recant the whole thing; take some solace in your booze.

I am no pope, nor a king. I cannot do as I choose.
Ptolemy and Aristotle got it right, and I did not.
And yet, it moves.

The whole of my philosophy, and all of my views:
you see, what I saw, well, it's a bit of a blind spot.
I did not intend to light this particular fuse.
But despite what I've said: yet, it moves.

# Letter to Heisenberg

You said that there was a fundamental limit
to the precision with which
we could measure the complimentary variables
of a particle simultaneously.
So, we can never know the exact position
and the exact speed of a thing contemporaneously.

We call this principle "uncertainty," which is
an interesting way of saying we cannot know what we know.
This, of course, becomes a metaphor
for all sorts of events, most of them
less interesting than both quantum mechanics
and the multifarious nature of things.

Therefore, Werner, I have begun to think that you heard
a music beyond sound, a music that lies beneath the natural world,
and perhaps the other world as well,
and the reality to which both point.
You were right: the first few sips of science lead to disbelief,
but God waits for you at the bottom of the glass.

# LETTER TO GANDHI

Yesterday, shortly after five in the afternoon, an atheist
shot three Muslims, Yusor and Razan Abu-Salha and Deah Barakat.
In North Carolina, a place called Chapel Hill,
they say he killed them over a parking spot.

Earlier this week, someone killed an American girl in Northern Syria.
Her name was Kayla and her kidnappers were curs, fractions of men.
She was travelling to a relief hospital but she looked like she
might have grown up down the street from me on Melody Lane.

And last week, in Aleppo, they invited children to watch
the immolation of a Jordanian pilot. These children danced in celebration.
And a young boy, watching the horror said, "If the pilot was here,
I would burn him by my hand. I wish I could capture pilots and burn them."

And here in Tejas, angry men and women marched, threatened and shouted
to insure their right to carry their guns for everyone to see. They want it well known
as they parade around like Somali warlords. They want to turn this whole nation
into the O.K. Corral, into a town so aptly named Tombstone.

Here is our descent into madness. This is our age: godly but faithless.
This is our uncertain hour. So, I know what you said about how and when
to struggle against a system of injustice. But how do we overcome
this entropy? Where do we lay our heads in Bedlam?

Let me hear from you soon, old friend.
I am so impatient with this tenebrous dread.
The dogs are tired,
and I am going to bed.

## RIO DA DÚVIDA

## I.

*Black care rarely sits behind a rider whose pace is fast enough.*
—Theodore Roosevelt

I can still see you standing there in early October, 1913,
At Pier 8 in Brooklyn on the *Vandyck*.
You shook your own hands and grinned
at the well-wishers and gawkers.
You were all teeth and spectacles in those days.

You were no man for an old country and
set out to explore the unseen jungles,
to go beyond every hint of the maps,
full of bluster and bravado, to lick your wounds and
piece together the remains

of your life, the scraps. You habitually
left behind loss and shame and sorrow—
after your father died in the wilderness of Oyster Bay,
and you high-tailed it for the Badlands of the Dakotas
after that terrible day when all the lights dimmed.

And I don't think you were running away from the pain
as much as you sought to skirt the eddy of despondency,
to skedaddle from the sadness you feared would consume you.
I think you knew that, like one of your insect specimens,
You would be pinned

against this heartache. And so, shortly before the world
began to gather the materiel, to bundle up the madness
necessary for the war it would call great, you left
seeking consolation in Brazil,
running from defeat and loss.

49

And it's bully for you, and it's bully for me.
sailing beyond rhyme, beyond reason:
a geographical tour, a naturalist's allure,
in the height of the rainy season.


II.


*Colonel Roosevelt, why don't you go down an unknown river?*
—Lauro Müller


Upon arriving in Brazil, you met your son,
flesh of your flesh and bone of your bone.
He was thin and fair, an engineer:

the most sensitive of your children, with a history
of malarial fevers. Kermit had always bird-dogged
your affection, your imprimatur.

On December 12, you encountered the indomitable
Cândido Rondon, who would join you in leading this expedition,
this audacity. He knew the Amazon as well as any man alive.

This *mestizo*, this diminutive *caboclo*, had already
strung telegraph wire across the great wilderness
and had discovered the River of Doubt.

By the 19th of January, the expedition
was ready to depart Tapirapuã for the long odyssey
across the Brazilian highlands. Through fields and arid mesas,

through swarming jungles, the expedition began
to understand this place and its defiance.
At the end of the day, the men gathered around

the campfires, telling stories of past adventures,
of temples and strange beasts and terrible battles.
None told the tales better than you, the raconteur-in-chief.

You and the other colonel wandered into the *Mato Grosso,*
along the basin where the Amazon drains.
In search of *terra incognita,* you strolled off without regard

to poison darts, maribundi wasps, fevers, or a river full of pain.
By the time you reached Utiarity in late January of '14 the rations
began to wane, the tropical fevers took hold of your son, and

the sky let loose the rains. Circumstances required that the expedition
relieve itself of its volume. You shed yourself of one of the naturalists and
that meddlesome priest, "a very commonplace little fool." And still,

the headwaters of the River of Doubt lay in the distance:
beyond the hordes of gnats and "eye licker" bees,
beyond the relentless rain. The river lay beyond the surrender of the oxen,

the failure of the mules, beyond the baggage and boats
and provisions which you were compelled to abandon.
The *Rio da Dúvida* lay beyond the stone-age Nhambiquaras,

beyond their poison tipped arrows,
beyond the terror of the recognition that you
were being watched, that you were being followed.

The river lay beyond the Brazilian soldiers you found
buried in the sand, shoulders and heads
rising up from the ground. For all these things, you were unprepared.

And it's bully for you, and it's bully for me,
for this life, this adventure, is never banal.
We're off to explore, to map more and more,
with the lord of the Panama canal.

# III.

*My father always wanted to be the corpse at every funeral, the bride*
*at every wedding and the baby at every christening.*
—Alice Roosevelt

In February, you began your descent of the unforgiving black waters
of the River of Doubt, which wove through the ceaseless jungle
for a thousand miles. In the early going, the stunning beauty of the river
was inescapable: palm trees crowned like some *Magna Mater*
with blood-red orchids, deep green parakeets fluttering in the air,
and *Jesus Christo* birds walking on the water.

You began down the river with seven rough-hewn Nhambiquaran boats,
cumbersome and terribly heavy: a burden when it came to portage.
In the day, you heard the constant choir of birds and
the operatic howl of the monkeys as the cicadas joined in the din.
And in the evenings, the shrill cry of crickets commenced at sunset:
a pristine world, predating and resisting the botanist's ken.

The black flies and mosquitoes swarmed you
in this strange and deadly geography. Venomous snakes,
poison frogs, immense anacondas, the primordial cayman,
the ravenously savage piranha, the parasitic candiru, packs of wild pigs
and furtive jaguars all made their home on the River of Doubt. In this land
of tooth and claw, you were an unwelcome visitor, an uninvited transient.

The boatmen and porters, the *camaradas,* knew the rain forest.
They knew the way the light would eke through
the fractals of vines and leaves above and knew the ways
the bright, mottled butterflies would quiver over the river.
And they understood the quickening currents
and the distant roar of waterfalls and rapids.

The rapids and falls would sap the expedition's strength,
each requiring a portage of several days
as the *camaradas* slashed a trail through the jungle. In early March,
the pitiless river (and perhaps your ambition) claimed three of the canoes
and the life of the noble Simplicio. It nearly took your son.
As the river roiled, the food stores continued to wane.

Around then, you discovered that Colonel Rondon's dog
had been killed by the savage and superstitious Cinta Larga Indians.
They were predisposed to making war and ritual cannibalism.
The expedition was thus predisposed to vacating the premises,
some on the remaining boats, others hacking through the jungle:
all united in a common misery and desperation.

In late March, in the struggle against the rapids,
the quick current pinned two of the dugouts against
an assembly of boulders. Despite your feverish state,
You rushed into the river to wrench the canoes free before
they and the provisions were lost. You slipped and cut yourself
against a jagged rock, a bacterial invitation: a deadly auger.

And it's bully for you, and it's bully for me,
As the light begins to fade out.
There are no honors in these troubled waters,
not on the River of Doubt.

## IV.

*I have always thought it strange . . . how any man could be brought in close personal contact with Colonel Roosevelt without loving the man.*
—George Cherrie

The infection consumed you quickly,
thriving in the hot, moist tropical air,
conspiring with the malarial fevers.
You were then defined mostly by what you were not:
you were unable to rise from your cot and
unwilling to be carried about like a maharajah.

And so you asked that they leave you there. "You can get out.
I will stop here," you said. You intended to end your life, to drift away
with Morpheus and his uncle Thanatos. Your son,
however, convinced you that he could not and would not
leave you. The expedition continued on, despite the loss
of another canoe and the murder of the *camarada* Paishon.

The fever now seized hold of you, and you fell
into delirium, muttering that phrase again and again,
"In Xanadu did Kubla Khan a pleasure dome decree . . . .
In Xanadu did Kubla Khan a pleasure dome decree."
Exhausted and befuddled, you hobbled through the jungle,
through that unholy wilderness.

The daily rations amounted to a small portion of a poor man's meal,
at best. Nevertheless, you shared your measure with the porters.
You were more dead than alive in those days,
bearing this ordeal. Perhaps this was your Passion.
With your clothes in tatters, your gaunt figure
bore no resemblance to that happy imperialist you once were.

By mid-April, the swelling and pain of the infection
compelled a surgical intervention. The expedition's physician
cleaned and drained the abscess in the worst of all possible
surgical theatres as the pium and borrachudo flies gathered
at the wound. You kept your silence despite the pain.
By that point, only a fragment of you remained.

By the 26th of April, you saw two flags fluttering
in the breeze: the Brazilian and the American banners.
And while you would return to New York in mid-May,
you would never again be the man who so consistently punched
above his weight. No longer "a steam engine in trousers,"
you had become a sick, tired, old man who once was something more.

And it's bully for you, and it's bully for me.
What remains lacks most of the thrill.
I'll meet you tomorrow or the day after that
at the house on Sagamore Hill.

## Note to My Father

I found a photograph of you the other day.
You were riding a brown pony, the same horse
on which you rode to school and worked the ranch—the source
of that silly grin, before time and trial and trouble would toss it away.

In the picture, you feigned a steely determination
which that one-quarter giggle belied, although it seemed suitable
to that dusty landscape and the irrefutable
Double Mountain Fork of the Brazos River, a land without affectation.

Looking into your eyes, I am convinced
you were prepared to meet any opposition
(Comanche, rattlesnake or long division)
on a moment's notice: this much, your face evinced.

I would like to talk to that boy you were then, to warn him of the road ahead,
to caution him against strong drink and loose women.
But you would not have listened to me any more than I would listen
to you. We rode together, however. We lived our lives, and we buried our dead.

# About These Messages

I remember a drizzling rain the third time
I saw that guy, that far-fetched fellow,
and he gave me his phone number.
He told me never to call
if the sun wasn't shining,
leading me to wonder

exactly what he meant.
I thought he intended to say
he wouldn't be home in the evenings,
but he was talking about these daily rains
that we've been having around nine in the morning,
three in the afternoon. And just as I was leaving

the dim light fell through my kitchen window
and spread out across the floor
as my beloved might spread out in a Turkish bath—
and I lost my train of thought. Yesterday,
the word came to me that I should go to Nineveh
and warn them of the consequences, of the aftermath

that would surely follow. Upon my arrival,
however, they announced
that I was no sight for sore eyes.
Beginning the journey back home, I learned that
the library in Alexandria had been destroyed by fire: a universe
of books and scrolls within which we sought to gather and systematize

all that was known or knowable. And I wept.
A childhood friend sent a letter to inform me that
my secret identity has been revealed and I have been betrayed.
I do not know my adversaries.
I do not know their number or their names.
That information was not conveyed.

The smartest people in the world have announced
that our weather is changing, that we should expect
a more extreme climate, but I suspect we won't.
You could set your watch by these rains
that we've been having but most of the people I know
(and most of the people they know) don't.

I don't understand these messages at all. I have listened for some hidden
communiqué within the squawk of the emergency broadcast system.
I assume it's there. I'll go along to get along.
But I think we should use another language for a while, and then return
to our native tongue for the rites of birth and burial
and to teach our children right from wrong.

# Letter to a Musician

We have been detained in these years,
old friend, but we keep the tune in mind.
When will you speak to me of your childhood
among the Tennessee wildflowers and legumes?

My mind, a wildflower too variegated
to grow among the others, but we
can still converse. Sometimes hearing
the mariachi band of drunken peasants

on the plaza and at others the antiphonal choir,
I think I will quit the orchestra and take up the ocarina,
carrying it in a purple bag bordered in passementerie.
Music is anything which lingers on and passes the time.

Can I set aside the silver tromba and the wrinkled white shirt
for the writhing terra cotta goose pipe—wandering out into the hills,
beyond the city and the civilized to look for the light
that does not dim, to listen for the song that does not fade away?

# LETTER TO AN OLD SPANIARD

Miguel, this morning, riding across the Pedernales River,
I thought of you, old friend, and of the struggle
against incivility. And I recalled the fierce battle
waged by that ingenious gentleman
against the giants. (Were they windmills?
No, they *were* giants.)

And I thought of your commitment,
your wise and honorable pledge
that you would tell the story
with absolutely no deviation from the truth.
And I propose to you a certain bargain:
that I will do the same.

I recalled how that mad old knight
and his brave horse were removed from the earth,
And then flung back down again,
shattered, bruised, broken and unbalanced.
He thrust his hands, all the way to his elbows,
into the pursuit of adventure and decency.

But this morning, I am in no peril.
I have never seen this country, my home, so green.
The congregation of false daisies, bitterweed,
Indian paintbrush and bluebonnets rise up,
reaching for the cerulean sky like hundreds
of thousands of gospel singers in praise.

No, I am in no peril today,
nor will I set about any righteous warfare this morning.
For me, the grace of West Texas in spring
and today's wildflowers will suffice.
And this morning, those ragged pickpockets
of yesterday and tomorrow will not unhorse me.

# CONVERSATION WITH THE MUSE

You stumble through this European castle in the dark
while I'm trying to get some sleep. You are fashionably

late as usual, bringing me all these souvenirs—
pillow slips from Iceland and hambone from Peru.

I wonder what can be withstood, and
where is the harmonica I'd requested.

We called you Genesis or Genitalia;
those names way and wink. Touching

everything in sight, they cripple us,
remove our clothing, and change us

into birds. Now we understand
not to call you that anymore.

      Forget about the harmonica, and answer a few questions.
      Why are you reading so much of the historic lately

      and which bath oils are best among these?
      Look at me, I was insulted three times

      And never spoke of it.
      You foreigners complain too much.

      To compound our troubles,
      you have misquoted me.

The odd daughter of memory,
You go on clattering and bumping,

through these dark continental hallways,
late and unusual.

# THE *SULTANA* DISASTER

*Estimates ran as high as 1800 dead and presumed dead,*
*with 1585 as the figure most generally agreed upon. That was more than the number*
*killed on both sides at the first Bull Run and Wilson's Creek combined,*
*and even by the lowest count the loss of the Sultana went into the books as the*
*greatest maritime disaster of all time.*
—Shelby Foote

They boarded in Vicksburg, not long after
the pistol shot interrupted the drama.
These ragged, skeletal, empty men
had been held at Andersonville and Cahaba.

The pistol shot having cut short the drama,
the ship spread the news along a flood-swollen Mississippi.
These fragments of men had been held at Andersonville and Cahaba,
stretching the steamboat to six times her capacity.

The ship spread the wretched news along a war-weary Mississippi,
but just south of Vicksburg a boiler began to leak.
There, the ship took on her frail cargo,
and a meager patch placed upon a failing seam.

Just south of Vicksburg, when the boiler began to leak,
hurried, haphazard repairs were effected.
A patch of lesser thickness was applied over the gibbous seam
and twenty-one hundred broken men expected

to go someplace like home, once the hurried, haphazard repairs were effected.
North, anyplace north of those beastly camps, those islands of hell:
that's what twenty-one hundred tattered men expected.
And "going home": the sorcery of those words cast an insurmountable spell.

Anywhere north of those pestiferous camps, those islands of hell,
shone like a fool's paradise, a mirage in the watery distance.
And twenty one hundred broke-down men expected
to be repatriated, to navigate up the waters of least resistance.

Drawn to the fool's paradise, steaming upstream into the watery distance
they cheered as they got underway, certain that their troubles were past.
Returning home, traveling up the river of least resistance,
prisoners of a war they called Civil: headed home, home at last.

Cheering when underway, or as much of a cheer as they could amass,
they barely noticed as the decks began to sag and creak.
These prisoners of a native conflict sailed for home, home at last.
The rebellious South all but conquered; the Union tired of their pique.

They hardly noticed the decks which, under their load, began to sag and creak
as inflamed boilers struggled against the distended waterway.
The crumbling South lay nearly conquered; the Union weary of its pique.
And the Mississippi, which offered moment's hope, would lead them all astray.

The inflamed boilers strained against the bitterly cold waterway
which overflowed her banks and enveloped most of the trees.
And the Mississippi, the Great River, would lead these vagrant men astray.
The muddy water rose around them, spreading across the land like some disease.

The river spilled across her banks and reached the highest branches,
she bore them to Memphis, where the *Sultana* took on bituminous coal.
The dirty water rose around them, pushing back the steamship, resisting her advances.
The paddle wheel compelled her into the night, carrying away all those souls.

Having borne those brittle men to Memphis, the *Sultana* acquired more coal.
The ship set out for Cairo at midnight, and while her passengers struggled to rest
the paddle wheel slapped the water into the night and ferried along those souls.
And then, one by one, the boilers began to confess

their faults two hours past midnight, while those pallid pilgrims
struggled to rest. Then fire and steam rose from up from perdition
as one by one, the three boilers began to confess
their failures: Gehenna requiring no further definition.

The fire and steam rose up, advancing from perdition.
Flames swallowed men and structure
and their failures. The fires of Gehenna needed no further definition.
Men were tossed into the river, and clung together in clusters.

While fire and steam consumed structure and soul
the screams faded into moans as the current swept them away.
Father, brother, son: tossed in the river, clinging in clusters,
then letting go as their strength gave way.

Scream dimmed to moan as the current bore them away.
Seventeen hundred perished. Leaving the war, having finished their atonement,
letting go, as their strength would give way.
They probably missed the irony of the moment.

# A Simple Poem

This is a simple poem. It shuns complications.
I use the term "complications" in the medical sense:
an adverse reaction to a procedure, a foreign substance, or an event.

This is a religious poem. Reciting the Liturgy of the Hours,
each syllable calls out for holiness. This poem has taken vows
of poverty, purity, and obedience.

This is an English poem, by which I don't mean the language
(which is obvious). Rather, I mean its respect for Her Majesty,
the Union Jack, and its gin-soaked dreams of an empire gone by.

Within this poem, you find yourself lost in a wilderness
of superstition: conspiracy theories, gypsy curses, horseshoes,
astrology, a witching wand, and protections from the evil eye.

This poem has soporific qualities. It will combat the
sleeplessness we encounter, and the night terrors, too.
Like poppies, it lulls us, it compels us, to sleep, sleep, sleep.

This is a seductive poem. The words hang a little too loosely, cling
to the page a little too tightly, and wind themselves around you
as though they could fulfill your deepest needs.

This is a disappointing poem. While early on
it may have shown some potential, it will not rise
to the level of our expectations.

This poem is full of patriotic fervor. It beats the martial drums,
increases defense spending, parades about in uniform;
it fulminates and growls at the poems of other nations.

This poem is creepy: not like a horror movie, or a pandemic,
more like a stranger you catch a glimpse of three times in the same day,
almost out of sight. This poem has been following me and following you.

This is a musical poem, singing scat
into a moonless Harlem night. This poem improvises
on a theme, howling a lonesome doobie doobie do.

This poem has been involved with the Cosa Nostra, the Black Hand,
the mob. This poem will make you an offer you cannot refuse.
It will smile wryly through wine-stained teeth and call you *"paesan."*

This poem is a liar. You will not find the love of the truth on these pages.
This poem feigns indifference, as though it will not miss you
when you are gone.

ABOUT THE AUTHOR


JAMES R. DENNIS

IS A NOVELIST, A POET, AND A DOMINICAN FRIAR. ALONG WITH TWO FRIENDS,
HE IS CO-AUTHOR OF MILES ARCENEAUX MYSTERY SERIES. HE ALSO WRITES AND TEACHES
ON SPIRITUAL MATTERS. HE WAS BORN IN WEST TEXAS, AND LIVES IN
SAN ANTONIO WITH HIS TWO ILL-BEHAVED DOGS."

COLOPHON

CORRESPONDENCE IN D MINOR
WAS COMPOSED IN CLOISTER LIGHT, A TYPEFACE EVOLVED FROM THE
BLACKLETTER FONTS CREATED IN WESTERN EUROPE IN THE MID-TWELFTH CENTURY
AND USED BY JOHANNES GUTENBERG IN THE FIRST PRINTED BIBLES.
THE BARBED-WIRE CROSS REFERENCES A TATTOO STENCIL DRAWN BY PPUNKER FOR DEVIANT.
THE PAPER IS CRANES LETTRA, REICHPAPER'S SAVOY, AND CURIOUS MATTER.
LETTERPRESS HANDPRINTING IS BY WORKHORSE; PRINTING AND BINDERY ARE BY
RR DONNELLY. THE AUTHOR WAS PHOTOGRAPHED IN SAN ANTONIO'S
HISTORIC MENGER BAR BY DOROTHY TARBOX.
BOOK DESIGN IS BY LANA RIGSBY.

PUBLISHED BY STEPHEN F. AUSTIN STATE UNIVERSITY PRESS

Amor enim, sine qua nihil est.